500

MOST COMMON

LIST NEETPG

1st Edition

Tanmay K. Mehta

MBBS, MD, DNB, PCDCTM

Assistant Professor

Department of Microbiology

Smt. N.H.L. Municipal Medical College,

Ahmedabad

500 Most common list NEET PG

Website : www.Qworld.co.in

Email :qworld.co.in@gmail.com

Medical knowledge is constantly changing. The author, editors, contributors and the publisher have, as far as it is possible, taken care to ensure that the information given in this text is accurate and up-to-date. However, readers are strongly advised to confirm that the information complies with current legislation and standards of practice.

Print ISBN : 9781549545108

First edition : 2017

Published by : Qworld

1.Most common aortic branch involved in Takayasu arteritis : Left subclavian

2.Most common cause of respiratory distress in newborn : Transient tachypnea of the newborn

3.Most common location to see Asbestosis sequale : Posterior lower lobes

4.Most common karyotype / chromosomal abnormality in USA : Down's syndrome

5. Most common osseous lymphoma, primary and secondary : Diffuse large B-cell lymphoma

6. Most common primary malignant orbital tumor in childhood : Rhabdomyosarcoma

7. Most common type of fluid collection in scrotum : Hydrocele

8. Most common type of liposarcoma to affect children : Myxoid liposarcoma

9. Most common abdominal emergency of early childhood : Intussusception.

10. Most common acetabular fracture : Posterior acetabulum.

11. Most common affected bowel segment in TB : Ileocecal area.

12. Most common affected joint in gout : First MTP.

13. Most common AIDS-related neoplasm : Kaposi Sarcoma

14. Most common allergic aspergillosis syndrome : Allergic bronchopulmonary aspergillosis.

15. Most common anatomic variant of pancreas : Pancreas divisum

16. Most common anomalous course of RCA : Interarterial

17. Most common appearance of Legionella at the peak of the disease : Bilateral airspace consolidation.

18. Most common assoc. w/ Fx of great toe distal phalanx with physeal involvement :Osteomyelitis.

19. Most common associated anomaly with coarctation : Bicuspid valve.

20. Most common association of PAPVR : Sinus venosus type ASD.

21. Most common association with small left colon syndrome : Maternal DM

22. Most common bacterial cause of mesenteric adenitis : Yersinia enterocolitica.

23. Most common benign cardiac rhythm abnormality : PAC

24. Most common benign cartilage-containing tumor : Osteochondroma

25. Most common benign growth of the skeleton : Osteochondroma

26. Most common benign hepatic lesion : Hemangioma

27. Most common benign hepatic tumor during fist 6 mo. of life : Infantile Hemangioendothelioma

28. Most common benign intraconal tumor of the orbit in adults : Cavernous hemangiomas.

29. Most common benign masses caused by asbestos exposure : Atelectatic Asbestos Pseudotumor

30. Most common benign mesenchymal tumor of kidney : AML

31. Most common benign mucosal tumor of the esophagus : Papilloma

32. Most common benign nasopharyngeal tumor : Juvenile angiofibroma.

33. Most common benign orbital tumor in childhood : Dermoid Cyst of Orbit

34. Most common benign ovarian neoplasm in young and middle-aged women (<45 years) :Mature teratoma

35. Most common benign radiation-induced tumor of the musculoskeletal system : Osteochondroma

36. Most common benign rib lesion in an adult : Fibrous dysplasia.

37. Most common benign soft-tissue tumor of the foot : Plantar fibromatosis

38. Most common benign soft-tissue tumor of vascular origin : Hemangioma

39. Most common benign solid tumor in women of childbearing age : Fibroadenoma

40. Most common benign testicular mass : Simple cyst

41. Most common benign tumor of spleen : Hemangioma

42. Most common benign tumor of the larynx : Squamous papilloma

43. Most common benign tumor of the lung : Hamartoma

44. Most common benign tumor of the small bowel : GIST

45. Most common benign vascular gastric tumor : Glomus tumor of stomach.

46. Most common bilateral testicular tumor : Lymphoma

47. Most common biliary complication s/p lap. cholecystectomy : Bile duct leak from cystic duct stump.

48. Most common biliary complication s/p liver transplantation : Obstruction/stenosis at anastomosis.

49. Most common bladder neoplasm in children younger than 10 years : Rhabdomyosarcoma

50. Most common bone to develop an osteochondroma : Femur (tibia second most common)

51. Most common brain anomaly on prenatal sonograms : Isolated Mild Ventriculomegaly

52. Most common breast tumor under age 25 years : Fibroadenoma

53. Most common cardiac manifestation of Systemic Lupus Erythematous : Pericarditis

54. Most common cardiac tumor in children : Rhabdomyoma.

55. Most common cardiac valvular tumor : Papillary fibroelastoma

56. Most common carpal dislocation : Transscaphoid perilunate dislocation.

57. Most common causative organism of acute pyogenic meningitis in adults : Strep. pneumoniae

58. Most common causative organism of neonatal pyogenic meningitis : E. coli

59. Most common cause for failure of dialysis graft : Fibrointimal hyperplasia : venous outflow stenosis.

60. Most common cause for late failure in lung transplant patient : Bronchiolitis obliterans

61. Most common cause for pulmonary edema : Left-sided heart disease

62. Most common cause non iatrogenic cause of small bowel obstruction : Hernia

63. Most common cause of a large choroid plexus cyst : Trisomy 18.

64. Most common cause of a large pleural fluid collection in the newborn period : Chylothorax

65. Most common cause of acute renal failure in children requiring dialysis : HUS

66. Most common cause of acute testicular pain in postpubertal male : Acute epididymitis

67. Most common cause of acute testicular pain in prepubertal male : Torsion

68. Most common cause of AIDS cholangiopathy : Cryptosporidium

69. Most common cause of an echogenic renal mass in a 3-month-old : Mesoblastic nephroma.

70. Most common cause of an intraorbital mass lesion in adult : Pseudotumor of Orbit

71. Most common cause of AS in Western world : Degenerative disease

72. Most common cause of bilateral breast edema : CHF.

73. Most common cause of bilateral echogenic renal cortex : Chronic glomerulonephritis.

74. Most common cause of biliary obstruction : Choledocholithiasis

75. Most common cause of bleeding between menstrual cycles : Endometrial hyperplasia.

76. Most common cause of bronchopneumonia : Staphylococcal

77. Most common cause of cancer deaths in males and females : Bronchogenic Carcinoma

78. Most common cause of cause of infectious esophagitis : Candida Esophagitis

79. Most common cause of cavitary (necrotic) pneumonia in a child : Strep pneum.

80. Most common cause of Charcot joints : Diabetes mellitus

81. Most common cause of CHF in a child : ALCAPA / aberrant left coronary artery

82. Most common cause of CHF in a neonate : Hypoplastic Left Heart.

83. Most common cause of chronic hydronephrosis in renal transplant : UV anastomosis stricture.

84. Most common cause of colonic obstruction in adults : Malignancy

85. Most common cause of colonic obstruction in the infant : Meconium plug syndrome in CF patients

86. Most common cause of colovesical fistula : Diverticulitis

87. Most common cause of congenital CNS infection : CMV.

88. Most common cause of congenital duodenal obstruction : Duodenal atresia.

89. Most common cause of congenital sensorineural hearing loss : Giant vestibular aqueduct syndrome

90. Most common cause of cord ischemia : Thromboembolic disease

91. Most common cause of coronary artery aneurysm in USA : Atherosclerosis

92. Most common cause of coronary artery aneurysm Worldwide : Kawasaki

93. Most common cause of cyanosis in a child : Tetralogy of Fallot

94. Most common cause of cyanosis n newborn Transposition of great vessels

95. Most common cause of death in a severe pelvic fracture : Hemorrhage.

96. Most common cause of death in Ataxia – Telangiectasia : Respiratory failure.

97. Most common cause of death in Jeune syndrome : Respiratory failure

98. Most common cause of drop mets : Medulloblastoma

99. Most common cause of dwarfism : Achondroplasia

100. Most common cause of echogenic renal pyramids in children : Furosemide

101. Most common cause of ejaculatory duct obstruction : Mullerian duct cyst ?

102. Most common cause of endometriosis in girls <16 years of age : Obstructive müllerian duct anomalies

103. Most common cause of end-stage renal disease : Diabetic Nephropathy

104. Most common cause of epididymitis in males aged 15 to 35 years : Sexually transmitted diseases

105. Most common cause of esophageal rupture : Iatrogenic

106. Most common cause of exocrine pancreatic insufficiency in patients <30 years of age : CF

107. Most common cause of facial hemipalsy : Bell palsy

108. Most common cause of false-positive V/Q scan for acute PE : Previous pulmonary embolism

109. Most common cause of fungal infection in AIDS patients : Cryptococcosis

110. Most common cause of gastrocolic fistula : Gastric ulcer.

111. Most common cause of heart failure in patients with COPD : Atherosclerotic heart disease

112. Most common cause of hemifacial spasticity is vertebrobasilar dolichoectasia.

113. Most common cause of hepatic calcifications : Infection

114. Most common cause of hydronephrosis in the newborn male : Ureteropelvic junction

115. Most common cause of hyperreflexive bladder : Spinal cord trauma

116. Most common cause of increased nuchal thickness : Downs syndrome

117. Most common cause of interstitial and airspace edema : CHF

118. Most common cause of intradiaphragmatic cyst :Extralobar sequestration

119. Most common cause of intraventricular hemorrhage :Disruption of the subependymal veins

120. Most common cause of intussusception in children >6 years : Lymphoma

121. Most common cause of large spherical pancreatic calcifications in children : Hereditary pancreatitis

122. Most common cause of left atrial dilatation : Mitral regurgitation.

123. Most common cause of leukokoria : Retinoblastoma.

124. Most common cause of liver metastasis : Colon.

125. Most common cause of lower extremity venous valve dysfunction : DVT.

126. Most common cause of lower GI bleeding : Diverticulosis.

127. Most common cause of malignancy of men in the world -- Bronchogenic Carcinoma

128. Most common cause of maternal peripartum death : Amniotic fluid embolism

129. Most common cause of membranous croup : Staph. Aureus.

130. Most common cause of microcolon: Meconium ileus.

131. Most common cause of mortality in ulcerative colitis : Toxic megacolon.

132. Most common cause of necrolytic migrating erythema : Glucagonoma

133. Most common cause of neonatal nasal obstruction : Choanal atresia.

134. Most common cause of Neonatal Pneumonia : Group B streptococcus.

135. Most common cause of neonatal respiratory distress in full term/postmature infants – Meconium aspiration

136. Most common cause of nephrocalcinosis in adults : Primary hyperparathyroidism

137. Most common cause of non-immune hydrops in USA : Cardiac anomaly

138. Most common cause of optic nerve enlargement : Optic nerve glioma

139. Most common cause of orbital calcifications : Retinoblastoma

140. Most common cause of orbital infection : Paranasal sinusitis

141. Most common cause of osteoblastic bone metastases in an adult female : Breast cancer

142. Most common cause of osteoblastic bone metastases in an adult male : Prostate cancer

143. Most common cause of osteolytic bone metastases in a child : Neuroblastoma

144. Most common cause of osteolytic bone metastases in an adult female : Breast cancer

145. Most common cause of osteolytic bone metastases in an adult male : Lung cancer

146. Most common cause of Osteomyelitis of spine : Penetrating direct trauma

147. Most common cause of pancreatic lipomatosis in children : CF

148. Most common cause of pleural eosinophilia : Air in the pleural space

149. Most common cause of pneumoperitoneum : Ruptured duodenal ulcer.

150. Most common cause of postpartum fever : Endometritis.

151. Most common cause of pseudomyxoma peritonei : Appendiceal mucinous adenocarcinoma

152. Most common cause of pseudoureterocele : Bladder tumor

153. Most common cause of pulmonary hypoplasia : Diaphragmatic hernia

154. Most common cause of pulmonary tumor embolus : Gastric carcinoma

155. Most common cause of recurrent hip disloc. s/p hip arthroplasty : Acetabular component malposition

156. Most common cause of reflux in child w/ non-duplicated collecting system: Short intramural ureter.

157. Most common cause of renal vein thrombosis in adults : Nephrotic syndrome

158. Most common cause of restrictive cardiomyopathy : Amyloid

159. Most common cause of round pneumonia in children : Streptococcus.

160. Most common cause of round pneumonia in children : Streptococcus

161. Most common cause of small bowel obstruction : Adhesions

162. Most common cause of squamous cell ca. in the renal pelvis : Chronic Infected stag horn calculus

163. Most common cause of stridor in neonate and young infant : Laryngomalacia

164. Most common cause of sudden cardiac death among young people Hypertrophic cardiomyopathy (HCM)

165. Most common cause of SVC syndrome : Bronchogenic carcinoma

166. Most common cause of testicular swelling : Hydrocele

167. Most common cause of the pulmonary-renal syndrome : Microscopic polyangitis.

168. Most common cause of the stripe sign on V/Q scan : COPD

169. Most common cause of thoracic outlet syndrome : Scalene anticus.

170. Most common cause of toxic mega colon : Pseudomembranous colitis.

171. Most common cause of tree in bud appearance on CT : Bronchiolitis

172. Most common cause of tricuspid stenosis : Rheumatic heart disease

173. Most common cause of unilateral diaphragmatic paralysis : Malignant invasion

174. Most common cause of unilateral nonperfused lung on V/Q scan : Bronchogenic carcinoma

175. Most common cause of unilateral pulmonary edema : Prolonged unilateral dependent positioning

176. Most common cause of urinary obstruction in boys : posterior urethral valves

177. Most common cause of valvular heart disease in the United States : Degenerative

178. Most common cause of vascular ring : Double arch.

179. Most common cause of vertebra plana in children : EG

180. Most common cause requiring bronchial artery embolization : CF

181. Most common cause worldwide for cholangiocarcinoma : Clonorchis sinensis infestation

182. Most common cerebellar neoplasm in children : Medulloblastoma

183. Most common cerebral mass lesion in AIDS : Toxoplasmosis

184. Most common chest radiograph finding seen in pts with an acute PE : Atelectasis

185. Most common chest x-ray abnormality in the ICU : Atelectasis

186. Most common child abuse facture : Diaphyseal fracture,

187. Most common collagen disorder for a pleural effusion : SLE

188. Most common colonic polyp : Hyperplastic polyp

189. Most common colonic site for lymphoma : Cecum

190. Most common complication of ERCP : Pancreatitis

191. Most common complication of popliteal artery aneurysm : Distal ischemia (thrombosis/embolism)

192. Most common complication with IVC filters : DVT.

193. Most common component of mixed germ cell tumors : Embryonal Cell Carcinoma

194. Most common congenital abnormality of GI tract : Meckel's diverticulum

195. Most common congenital anomaly of CNS in live births : Myelomeningocele

196. Most common congenital defect of CNS : Anencephaly.

197. Most common congenital head and neck cyst in a child : Thornwaldt cyst

198. Most common congenital heart disease : Bicuspid aortic valve.

199. Most common congenital intracranial tumor : Epidermoid or inclusion cyst

200. Most common congenital lesion of bile ducts : Choledochal Cyst

201. Most common congenital skeletal dysplasia : Achondroplasia.

202. Most common congenital solid tumor in the newborn : Sacrococcygeal Teratoma (1:40K live births)

203. Most common cranial nerve affected by a pituitary macroadenoma : CN VI.

204. Most common cranial nerve to be affected with schwannoma : VIII

205. Most common craniofacial malformation : Facial Clefting

206. Most common crystalline arthropathy : CPPD

207. Most common CT finding in bowel ischemia : Bowel wall thickening.

208. Most common cyanotic congenital heart malformation beyond neonatal period : TOF

209. Most common cyst of the jaw : Radicular cyst = Periapical cyst

210. Most common cystic lesion of prostate : Cystic degeneration of BPH

211. Most common cystic tumor of pancreas : Mucinous cystic neoplasm

212. Most common diffuse breast disorder : Fibrocystic disease of breast.

213. Most common diffuse gray matter degenerative disease : Alzheimer's

214. Most common dislocated auditory ossicle longitudinal temporal bone fracture : Incus

215. Most common dislocation in adult : Glenohumeral.

216. Most common dislocation in child : Elbow.

217. Most common epididymal neoplasm : Adenomatoid tumor

218. Most common estrogenic ovarian tumor : Granulosa Cell Tumor

219. Most common etiology for chronic temporal lobe epilepsy : Ganglioglioma

220. Most common etiology for multiple small gastric polyps : Hyperplastic polyps.

221. Most common etiology for osteomyelitis : Staphylococcus aureus.

222. Most common etiology of bilaterally enlarged, hyperechoic kidneys in newborn infant : ARPKD.

223. Most common etiology of mesenteric adenitis : Viral

224. Most common etiology of pneumomediastinum : Alveolar rupture.

225. Most common etiology of rickets : Vitamin D deficiency.

226. Most common extra-adrenal site of pheochromocytoma : Organ of Zuckerkandl.

227. Most common extraaxial neoplasm of CNS : Meningioma

228. Most common extragonadal site of primary germ cell tumors : Anterior mediastinum.

229. Most common extrapulmonary site of tuberculosis : Urinary tract

230. Most common fetal cardiac anomaly seen on 4 chamber view US : AV canal defect (aka ECD)

231. Most common fibromatosis in childhood : Infantile Myofibromatosis

232. Most common finding of a tubal pregnancy seen on US images Adnexal mass separate from ovary

233. Most common finding of contralateral kidney in MCKD : Reflux

234. Most common fluid collection seen in transplant patients : Lymphoceles.

235. Most common form of aortic stenosis : Valvular

236. Most common form of carpal instability : DISI

237. Most common form of emphysema in alpha-1 antitrypsin deficiency : Panlobular emphysema

238. Most common form of emphysema in nonsmokers : Panlobular emphysema

239. Most common form of emphysema in smokers : Centrilobular emphysema

240. Most common form of hypertrophic cardiomyopathy : Asymmetric involvement of the interventricular septum

241. Most common form of skeletal dysplasia : Acquired skeletal dysplasia.

242. Most common form of systemic vasculitis in adults : Giant cell (temporal) arteritis

243. Most common fracture of forearm : Colles

244. Most common functional tumors of the ovary : Sex cord–stromal tumors

245. Most common fungal infection in AIDS : Cryptococcus.

246. Most common genitourinary organ affected by neurofibromas : Urinary bladder

247. Most common germ cell tumor associated with excessive hCG production :Choriocarcinoma.

248. Most common germ cell tumor associated with excessive hCG production after choriocarcinoma : Dysgerminoma.

249. Most common GI neoplasm : Adenoma

250. Most common GI tract location for primary extranodal lymphoma : Stomach, usually NHL type.

251. Most common glial tumor in adults : Ependymoma

252. Most common glial tumor in NF 1 : JPA.

253. Most common glial tumor with microcalcifications : Oligodendroglioma

254. Most common gynecologic neoplasm : Uterine Leiomyoma

255. Most common hereditary hypercoagulable condition : Factor V Leiden

256. Most common hereditary leukodystrophy : Metachromatic leukodystrophy

257. Most common histologic type of bronchogenic carcinoma associated with cavitation : Squamous

258. Most common histologic type of bronchogenic carcinoma associated with pancoast tumor : Squamous

259. Most common histologic type of bronchogenic carcinoma associated with pleural effusion : Adenocarcinoma

260. Most common histologic type of lung cancer associated with asbestosis exposure : BAC

261. Most common histologic type of primary cutaneous lymphoma :T-cell lymphoma

262. Most common ILD to be found in association with collagen vascular disease : NSIP

263. Most common indication for percutaneous vertebroplasty : Osteoporosis.

264. Most common infection to cause cerebellar hypoplasia & migration anomalies : CMV

265. Most common infratentorial neoplasm in an adult : Metastases

266. Most common inherited disease among Caucasian Americans : CF

267. Most common internal enhancement pattern in DCIS with non mass like enhancement : Clumped enhancement

268. Most common intracranial for site of teratomas : Pineal region.

269. Most common intracranial presentation of TB : Tuberculous meningitis.

270. Most common intramedullary spinal neoplasm in adults : Ependymoma of Spinal Cord

271. Most common intramedullary tumor in children : Astrocytoma

272. Most common intramedullary tumor of adults : Ependymoma.

273. Most common intraocular neoplasm in childhood : Retinoblastoma

274. Most common intraorbital tumors found in adults : Cavernous hemangiomas.

275. Most common intrathoracic fetal anomaly : Congenital diaphragmatic Hernia

276. Most common intrathoracic foregut cyst : Bronchogenic Cyst

277. Most common intrauterine CNS infection : CMV

278. Most common intravascular venous tumor : Leiomyosarcoma of IVC

279. Most common in-utero renal tumor : Mesoblastic nephroma.

280. Most common invasive gynecologic malignancy : Endometrial malignancy

281. Most common islet cell tumor in MEN 1 : Gastrinoma

282. Most common islet cell tumor of the pancreas : Insulinoma.

283. Most common joint involved in synovial osteochondromatosis : Knee

284. Most common lesion to cause expansion of paranasal sinus : Mucocele

285. Most common lethal bone dysplasia : Osteogenesis imperfecta type II ?

286. Most common liver tumor after metastases : Hemangioma

287. Most common lobe affected in bronchial atresia : Left upper lobe.

288. Most common location for a cephalhematoma : Parietal

289. Most common location for a gastric diverticulum : Posterior wall of the gastric fundus.

290. Most common location for a pilocytic astrocytoma : Cerebellum

291. Most common location for a solitary myeloma of the bone : Thoracolumbar spine

292. Most common location for a synovial sarcoma : Knee

293. Most common location for a Tarlov cyst : Posterior rootlets of S2 + S3

294. Most common location for abdominal sarcoid involvement : Stomach

295. Most common location for atelectatic asbestos pseudotumor : Posteromedial & - lateral basal region of lower lobes

296. Most common location for chordomas : Sacral spine.

297. Most common location for gallbladder perforation : Fundus

298. Most common location for Sclerosing Osteomyelitis of Garré (sterile Osteomyelitis) : Mandible

299. Most common location for typhlitis : Cecum.

300. Most common location for well-differentiated liposarcoma : Thigh

301. Most common location in biliary tree for cholangiocarcinoma : Upper third/perihilar region.

302. Most common location in the spine for an osteochondroma : Cervical (C2) followed by thoracic T8

303. Most common location of a meningioma in the spine : Thoracic spinal cord

304. Most common location of a periurethral diverticulum in a female : Posterolateral.

305. Most common location of an ectopic pregnancy : Ampullary region of the fallopian tube.

306. Most common location of benign and malignant masses in breast : Upper outer quadrant

307. Most common location of bronchogenic carcinoma : Right upper lobe

308. Most common location of coarctation : Postductal beyond the origin of the left subclavian artery.

309. Most common location of coronary calcifications : LAD.

310. Most common location of DAI : Frontotemporal gray–white matter junction.

311. Most common location of GIST : Stomach.

312. Most common location of GU obstruction in a neonatal male : Ureteropelvic junction.

313. Most common location of intracranial dissection : Vertebral arteries.

314. Most common location of intraorbital abscess : Subperiosteal space on medial wall.

315. Most common location of intraventricular meningioma : Atrium of the lateral ventricle.

316. Most common location of oligodendroglioma : Frontal lobe.

317. Most common location of pleomorphic xanthoastrocytoma : Temporal lobes.

318. Most common location of pulmonary sequestration : Posterior medial lower.

319. Most common location of PVNS : Knee.

320. Most common location of sarcoidosis in spinal cord : Cervical.

321. Most common location of the biliary embryonal Rhabdomyosarcoma : CBD

322. Most common location of triquetral fracture is dorsal avulsion

323. Most common location to find a lithopedion : Adnexae

324. Most common location to see intravertebral vacuum phenomenon (Kümmell Disease) : Thoracolumbar junction

325. Most common lung infection in HIV: Bacterial pneumonia

326. Most common lung mass : Granuloma

327. Most common lysosomal storage disorder : Gaucher's disease

328. Most common malformation associated with callosal agenesis : Dandy-Walker malformation.

329. Most common malignancy of childhood : Leukemia.

330. Most common malignancy of parotid gland in adult : Mucoepidermoid carcinoma.

331. Most common malignant abdominal neoplasm in children 1–8 years old : Wilms Tumor.

332. Most common malignant bone tumor in children : Ewings

333. Most common malignant cause of bilateral global renal enlargement : Lymphoma.

334. Most common malignant neoplasm of diaphragm : Fibrosarcoma.

335. Most common malignant neoplasm of the spleen : Lymphoma.

336. Most common malignant ovarian neoplasm : Serous adenocarcinoma.

337. Most common malignant ovarian neoplasm : Serous cystadenocarcinoma.

338. Most common malignant primary bone tumor in young adults + children : Osteosarcoma

339. Most common malignant radiation-induced tumor of the musculoskeletal system : MFH

340. Most common malignant sex cord–stromal tumor : Granulosa cell tumor

341. Most common malignant testicular neoplasm : Nonseminomatous germ cell tumors

342. Most common malignant tumor affecting ribs of children + adolescents : Ewings Sarcoma

343. Most common malignant tumor of the abdomen in patients with NF1 Malignant peripheral nerve sheath tumor

344. Most common malignant tumor of the duodenum : Adenocarcinoma.

345. Most common malignant tumor of the heart : Angiosarcoma

346. Most common malignant tumor of the small bowel : Carcinoid

347. Most common mammographic finding in DCIS : Microcalcifications

348. Most common mammographic finding in Infiltrating/Invasive Lobular Carcinoma : Architectural distortion.

349. Most common manifestation of asbestosis exposure : Pleural plaques

350. Most common manifestation of asbestos-related pleural disease : Pleural effusion

351. Most common manifestation of blunt chest trauma : Pulmonary contusion

352. Most common mass lesion of the cerebellopontine angle after acoustic schwannoma : Meningioma

353. Most common mediastinal germ cell tumor : Seminoma.

354. Most common mediastinal mass in a child between the ages of 6 & 12 years old : Lymphoma

355. Most common mediastinal neurogenic tumor : Schwannoma

356. Most common mesenchymal origin neoplasm of GI tract : GIST

357. Most common metabolic liver disease in children : Hepatic cirrhosis in homozygous alpha-1 Antitrypsin Deficiency

358. Most common metastases to the spleen : Breast carcinoma

359. Most common metastasis to the heart : Melanoma

360. Most common metastatic cause of linitis plastica : Breast carcinoma

361. Most common metatarsal to have a stress fracture : Second metatarsal.

362. Most common missed type of breast cancer on mammography : Infiltrating/Invasive Lobular Carcinoma.

363. Most common mitral valve abnormality in the Western world : Non-rheumatic mitral valve disease.

364. Most common monodermal teratoma : Struma ovarii.

365. Most common motor neuron disease : ALS.

366. Most common MR imaging finding in DCIS : Non-masslike enhancement.

367. Most common mycotic pneumonia in an AIDS patient : Cryptococcus.

368. Most common natural outcome of the VSD : Spontaneous complete closure.

369. Most common neonatal cyanotic congenital heart malformation : TGV

370. Most common neonatal lesion of adrenal gland : Nontraumatic Adrenal Hemorrhage.

371. Most common neoplasm of conus medullaris : Myxopapillary Ependymoma of Spinal Cord.

372. Most common neoplasm of internal auditory canal / cerebellopontine angle : Vestibular Schwannoma.

373. Most common neoplasm of the gastrointestinal tract in patients with NF1: Neurofibromas.

374. Most common nerve to be involved in tarsal tunnel syndrome : Posterior tibial nerve.

375. Most common nonepidemic meningoencephalitis in immunocompetent individuals in US : Herpes Encephalitis.

376. Most common nonepithelial malignant bladder tumor : Leiomyosarcoma.

377. Most common nonepithelial tumor in the colon : Lipoma.

378. Most common nonepithelial tumor of the bladder : Leiomyoma.

379. Most common nonglial primary tumors of the central nervous system : Meningiomas.

380. Most common nonlymphoproliferative primary malignant tumor of the spine in adults : Chordoma.

381. Most common nonlymphoproliferative primary malignant tumor of the spine in children : PNET.

382. Most common nontraumatic cause of acute limp in a child : Toxic synovitis.

383. Most common non-traumatic cause of facial nerve paralysis & hearing loss : CPA tumor.

384. Most common odontogenic mass : Odontoma= odontogenic hamartomatous malformation.

385. Most common of all alimentary tract duplications : Small Bowel Duplication Cyst.

386. Most common of cerebral vascular malformation : DVA.

387. Most common opportunistic infection in AIDS : Toxoplasmosis.

388. Most common organism involved in pancreatic abscess : E. Coli.

389. Most common organism of acute pyogenic meningitis in infants & children : N. meningitides.

390. Most common origin of cystic artery : Right hepatic artery.

391. Most common osteochondrodysplasia : Hereditary Multiple Exostoses

392. Most common ovarian neoplasm : Dermoid aka dermoid cyst = Mature cystic teratoma

393. Most common ovarian tumor-related morbidity : Bowel obstruction

394. Most common pancreatic abnormality in adult pt's with CF : Complete fatty replacement

395. Most common paraneoplastic disease associated with thymoma : Myasthenia gravis

396. Most common parasitic infection involving CNS in developing countries : Cysticercosis

397. Most common parotid disease in children : Mumps parotitis

398. Most common pattern of bronchial arteries : Two left & one right bronchial artery

399. Most common pattern of enhancement at DE MR cardiac imaging : Patchy midwall enhancement with multiple foci

400. Most common pattern of hepatic involvement of secondary lymphoma : Diffuse infiltrative

401. Most common pattern of spread in Gallbladder Carcinoma : Direct spread.

402. Most common pediatric glioma : JPA

403. Most common pediatric tumor causing isosexual precocious puberty in a girl : Granulosa cell tumor

404. Most common phakomatoses : NF1

405. Most common pineal tumor : Pineal Germinoma

406. Most common predisposing cause to develop pneumothorax during percutaneous lung biopsy : COPD

407. Most common predisposing disorder of secondary spontaneous pneumothorax : COPD

408. Most common pregnancy-related mortality in the first trimester Ectopic pregnancy

409. Most common presentation for idiopathic pulmonary fibrosis : Dyspnea

410. Most common presentation in stuck twin syndrome : Monochorionic diamniotic

411. Most common presentation of bronchoalveolar cell carcinoma (BAC) : Solitary pulmonary nodule

412. Most common presentation of GIST on cross sectional imaging : Cystic areas of necrosis.

413. Most common presentation of mesoblastic nephroma : Palpable mass at birth.

414. Most common presentation of neurocysticercosis : Seizures.

415. Most common presenting symptom of Osler Weber Rendu : Hemoptysis.

416. Most common primary benign mesenteric tumor : Desmoid.

417. Most common primary brain tumor : GBM.

418. Most common primary cardiac tumors in adults : Myxomas.

419. Most common primary cerebellar mass in an adult : Hemangioblastoma

420. Most common primary demyelinating disease : MS

421. Most common primary female urethral malignancy : Squamous cell carcinoma

422. Most common primary hepatic neoplasm in infants & children <5 years old : Hepatoblastoma

423. Most common primary intraocular neoplasm in adult Caucasian : Uveal Melanoma

424. Most common primary lung tumor under age 16 : Bronchial Adenoma

425. Most common primary malignant rib tumor : Chondrosarcoma

426. Most common primary malignant sacral tumor : Sacrococcygeal Chordoma

427. Most common primary malignant soft-tissue tumor of late adult life : Soft-tissue MFH

428. Most common primary neoplasm of the spleen : Cavernous hemangioma

429. Most common primary neoplasms of the anterior superior mediastinum Thymomas.

430. Most common primary posterior mediastinal neoplasms :Neurogenic tumors

431. Most common primary tumor of the diaphragm : Lipoma

432. Most common radiation-induced CNS tumor : Meningioma

433. Most common reason for cardiac transplantation : Dilated cardiomyopathy

434. Most common recognized CNS manifestation of VHL disease : Hemangioblastoma of CNS

435. Most common relevant finding on cavogram for IVC filter placement : Circumaortic left renal vein.

436. Most common renal fusion anomaly : Horseshoe kidney

437. Most common renal mass in a 3 months old infant : Mesoblastic nephroma

438. Most common respiratory cause of cold agglutinin production : Mycoplasma pneumonia

439. Most common retinal infection in AIDS : Toxoplasmosis

440. Most common right cardiophrenic angle mass : Epicardial fat-pad/lipoma

441. Most common segment involved in tracheobronchial injury : Right lower lobe bronchus.

442. Most common sex cord-stromal cell tumor : Ovarian Fibroma

443. Most common sign of failing dialysis graft : Increased venous pressures

444. Most common sign of tuberous sclerosis : Myoclonic seizures

445. Most common single cause of breast lumps in females between 35 to 55 years of age : Breast cyst

446. Most common site for an intracardiac papillary fibroelastoma : Aortic valve.

447. Most common site for aneurysm in the chest : Descending thoracic aorta.

448. Most common site for cardiac myxoma : Left atrium

449. Most common site for intra cardiac thrombus formation : Atrial appendage.

450. Most common site for optic melanoma metastases : Liver.

451. Most common site for penetrating aortic ulcers : Descending thoracic aorta

452. Most common site of abdominal involvement in Hodgkins disease : Spleen

453. Most common site of aortic dissection : Prox. Desc. Thoracic aorta near ductus lig. attachment

454. Most common site of biliary tract injury caused by blunt abdominal trauma : Gallbladder

455. Most common site of monostotic fibrous dysplasia : Ribs

456. Most common site of rupture of sinus of Valsalva aneurysm : RV followed by RA.

457. Most common solid extracranial tumor of childhood : Neuroblastoma

458. Most common spermatic cord tumor : Lipoma

459. Most common spinal cord segment of lymphoma of spinal cord : Cervical

460. Most common spinal cord tumor : Ependymoma

461. Most common spinal location for cord astrocytoma : Thoracic

462. Most common spinal location for cord ependymoma : Cervical

463. Most common subcortical degenerative disease : Parkinson’s

464. Most common subglottic soft-tissue upper resp. tract obstructing mass in neonates : Subglottic Hemangioma

465. Most common submucosal tumor in colon : Lipoma

466. Most common subtype of NHL involving the esophagus : Diffuse large B-cell lymphoma

467. Most common subtype of renal cell carcinoma : Clear cell adenocarcinomas

468. Most common suprasellar mass : Craniopharyngioma

469. Most common syndromic islet cell tumor : Insulinoma

470. Most common systemic allergic hypersensitivity-related acute small-vessel vasculitis in children : HSP

471. Most common systemic fungal infection in immunocompromised patients : Candidiasis Of Liver

472. Most common tarsal bone to get fractured : Calcaneus

473. Most common tarsal coalition : Talocalcaneal

474. Most common testicular tumor in a young boy : Yolk sac tumor

475. Most common tibial plateau fractures : Lateral tibial plateau (Schatzker classification type I–III)

476. Most common trigonal intraventricular mass in adulthood : Meningioma

477. Most common tumor of adenohypophysis : Pituitary Adenoma

478. Most common tumor of genitourinary tract : Metachronous TCC

479. Most common tumor of the appendix : Carcinoid

480. Most common tumor of the esophagus : Leiomyomas

481. Most common tumor of the minor salivary glands : Adenoid Cystic Carcinoma

482. Most common type of abdominal wall hernia : Inguinal hernia

483. Most common type of ASD : Ostium secundum

484. Most common type of brain hernaition : anterior / uncal transtentorial

485. Most common type of brain herniation : Subfalcine herniation

486. Most common type of C2 fractures : Type 2

487. Most common type of cancer to arise from a thyroglossal duct cyst : Papillary carcinoma

488. Most common type of cardiomyopathy : Dilated cardiomyopathy

489. Most common type of choledochal cyst : fusiform dilatation of the extrahepatic duct Type 1c

490. Most common type of congenital internal hernia : Left paraduodenal hernia

491. Most common type of encephalocele in SE Asia: Sincipital Encephalocele

492. Most common type of encephalocele in US : Occipital Encephalocele

493. Most common type of endoleak in the abdominal aorta : Type II endoleak

494. Most common type of endoleak in the thoracic aorta : Type I endoleak

495. Most common type of fracture of the proximal 5th metatarsal bone : Peroneus brevis avulsion fracture.

496. Most common type of gallbladder inflammation : Chronic cholecystitis

497. Most common type of internal hernia : Postoperative, transmesenteric hernias.

498. Most common type of intrapulmonary involvement of Hodgkins disease : Bronchovascular form.

499. Most common type of liver abscess : Pyogenic Liver Abscess

500. Most common type of lymphoma involving the head and neck region : Diffuse large B-cell lymphoma

Printed in Great Britain
by Amazon

16911653R00061